People of Peace

40 inspiring icons

Sandrine Mirza & Le Duo

WIDE EYED EDITIONS

Building Peace

*T*hese women and men, enlightened thinkers, engaged citizens and revolutionary leaders, have all forcefully denounced the atrocity and absurdity of war, and fought against slavery, racial oppression and social injustice. They have spoken out against the violation of human rights everywhere with their rallying cry for non-violence.

Throughout the 20th century, which saw two world wars, a great deal of inhumanity, and the arrival of the nuclear bomb, these people left a lasting mark on their era. Some of them, such as Einstein, Gandhi, Martin Luther King, Picasso, and Mandela, have become worldwide icons.

But there are others you might not know about: Victor Schoelcher, who signed the decree abolishing slavery in France; Sophie Scholl, who was executed at the age of 21 for having denounced the Nazi regime; Jody Williams, who campaigned successfully against anti-personnel mines; and Rigoberta Menchú, who condemned the unjust treatment of Guatemalan Indians.

Their ideas and their actions have stood the test of time, as they embody positive values that are humanist, universal, and enduring. For everyone who dreams of a fairer and more united world, they are an endless source of inspiration. A better world. A peaceful world.

Contents

21

ELEANOR
ROOSEVELT

22

MARTIN LUTHER
KING

23

JOAN BAEZ

24

MUHAMMAD ALI

25

JOHN LENNON

26

ADOLFO PÉREZ
ESQUIVEL

27

MAIREAD CORRIGAN
AND BETTY WILLIAMS

28

WANGARI MAATHAI

29

IKUO HIRAYAMA

30

TENZIN GYATSO

31

MIKHAIL
GORBACHEV

32

VÁCLAV
HAVEL

33

NELSON MANDELA

34

RIGOBERTA
MENCHÚ

35

JODY WILLIAMS

36

DANIEL
BARENBOIM

37

KIM
DAE-JUNG

38

MICHAEL MOORE

39

TEGLA LOROUPE

40

MALALA YOUSAFZAI

Immanuel Kant

CONTEXT

This essay was published in 1795, not long after Prussia and revolutionary France had signed a peace treaty, and at a time when Europe was utterly weary of war.

Perpetual Peace is one of Immanuel Kant's most famous and most accessible essays. The German 18th-century philosopher's point of departure is the observation that states are either at war or living in a fragile peace; conflict is part and parcel of their nature. He felt that the law was the only way to put an end to this problem. The law of the strongest, Kant said, had to be replaced by a legal system that would regulate relations between the different states.

> **"Standing armies shall in time be totally abolished."**
>
> Immanuel Kant

IDENTITY

Philosopher, teacher

German

Born on April 22, 1724, in Königsberg (Prussia), now called Kaliningrad (Russia)

Died on February 12, 1804, in Königsberg

TO BE REPUBLICAN

Kant claimed that only a republic could guarantee peace, because it gave the people access to power. A republic refuses to engage in war, because it is the first to suffer the consequences, while monarchs do not hesitate to declare war because they can do so without putting themselves in danger.

HOSPITALITY

Kant felt that international law had to be based on hospitality: all people live on the same planet, and therefore have to support each other. When a stranger arrives in a country, she or he must not be treated as an enemy.

ACTION
Author of the philosophical essay: *Perpetual Peace*

ENLIGHTENED PHILOSOPHER
Kant was a leading figure in the movement called *des Lumières* (the Enlighteners).

WORKS
He wrote around 60 books, including the famous *Critique of Pure Reason*.

KÖNIGSBERG
Kant almost never left Königsberg, his native city, and is buried there.

The eminent philosopher

Victor Schoelcher

CONTEXT

The revolutionaries first abolished slavery in 1794, but Napoleon Bonaparte reintroduced it in 1802.

In 1828, Frenchman Victor Schoelcher traveled to Mexico, Florida, Louisiana, and Cuba on a business trip. He realized how appallingly the slaves there were treated, and became a leading figure in the abolitionist movement. Appointed undersecretary of the navy and the colonies as part of the provisional government of the brand-new Second Republic, he wrote the decree abolishing slavery in all French colonies signed on April 27, 1848. But the government rejected his proposal to compensate the former slaves and grant them plots of land.

25,000

black and mixed-race slaves were freed in Guadeloupe, Martinique, Guyana, Réunion, and Senegal

HUMANIST

Schoelcher also campaigned against the death penalty, for improving the status of women, and for protecting children. During the 1870 Franco-Prussian war, he declared his support for pacifism and an alliance of peoples.

SLAVERY

Slaves belonged to their masters, who made them work without pay. They were subjected to violence to make them fearful and obedient. They could be sold, hired out, given, exchanged—or emancipated (set free).

IDENTITY

Politician, journalist

French

Born on July 22, 1804, in Paris

Died on December 25, 1893, in Houilles

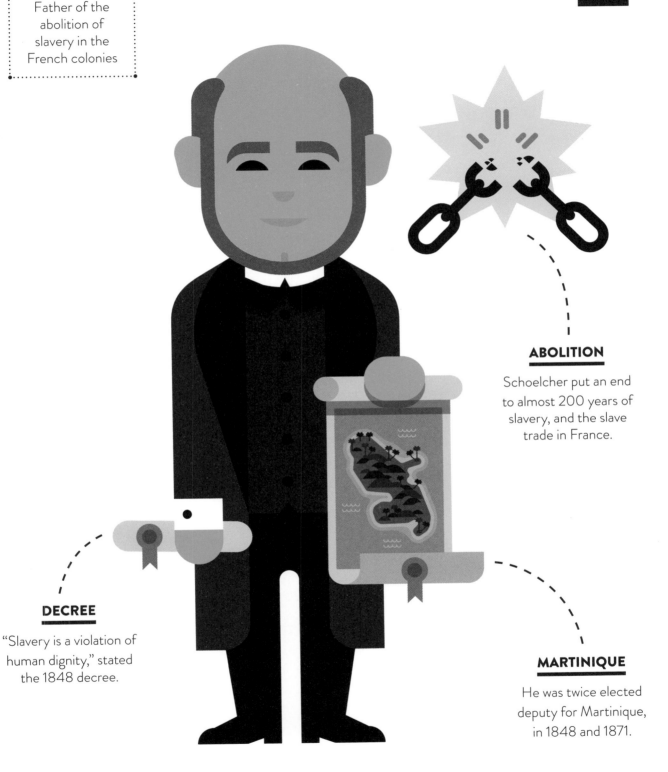

ABOLITION

Schoelcher put an end to almost 200 years of slavery, and the slave trade in France.

DECREE

"Slavery is a violation of human dignity," stated the 1848 decree.

MARTINIQUE

He was twice elected deputy for Martinique, in 1848 and 1871.

The opponent of slavery

Victor Hugo

CONTEXT

In Europe, the situation was explosive as one conflict after another broke out. Hugo wrote about the 1870 Franco-Prussian war in *L'Année terrible* (*The Terrible Year*).

One of the greatest ever French writers and political intellectuals, Victor Hugo was the president of the 1849 International Peace Congress, held in Paris during the Third Republic. It was at the Congress that he first talked about the idea of a United States of Europe. He called for a "European brotherhood" to be formed by all the continent's nations, including France, England, Germany, and Russia, explaining that they would trade and share ideas with each other instead of waging war. He is seen as the spiritual father of the European Union.

THE EXILE

Fiercely opposed to Napoleon III, who had seized power with a coup d'état, Hugo went into exile for over 19 years. However, he continued his opposition while in exile, publishing powerful pamphlets against the man he called "Napoleon the Little."

IDENTITY

Writer (novels, plays), poet, politician

French

Born on February 26, 1802, in Besançon

Died on May 22, 1885, in Paris

State funeral and burial at the Panthéon in Paris

HIS CAUSES

As well as war, Hugo denounced poverty, the oppression of women, the exploitation of children, hard labor, slavery, and the death penalty. These are the main themes of his famous novel, *Les Misérables*. He was a close friend of Victor Schoelcher.

> "A day will come when the bullets and the bombs will be replaced by votes."
>
> Victor Hugo to the 1849 Congress

ACTION
Speech on the United States of Europe at the International Peace Congress in 1849

EUROPE
"No more borders! The Rhine for all!" demanded Hugo in 1871.

POLITICAL WORKS
In 1849, Hugo wrote his celebrated speech on destroying extreme poverty.

PROMOTING PEACE
At the age of 67, he was honorary president of the Congress for Peace that took place in 1869, in Lausanne.

The visionary writer

Henry David Thoreau

Henry David Thoreau was an anti-conformist and anti-establishment American writer. In 1846, he chose to go to prison rather than pay his taxes to a government that accepted slavery of black people and the Mexican war. In the end, he only spent one night in prison, but as a result of this experience, he published his famous essay, *Civil Disobedience*, in 1849. It was the first text to put forward the theory of passive resistance, and was a source of inspiration to many people, including Mahatma Gandhi and Martin Luther King.

EDUCATION

Thoreau studied at Harvard University before becoming a teacher. But he resigned because he refused to administer corporal punishment to the students.

IDENTITY

Writer, naturalist

American

Born on July 12, 1817, in Concord, MA

Died on May 6, 1862, in Concord, MA

ABOLITIONIST

Thoreau helped slaves flee to Canada. He even defended John Brown, a supporter of armed struggle, who was arrested after encouraging an uprising among the slaves. But despite his efforts, the man was hanged.

ENVIRONMENTAL POET

At the age of 28, Thoreau decided to live alone, in a cabin in the middle of the forest. He described this two-year experiment in his book, *Walden; or, Life in the Woods*, an ode to nature, simple living, and freedom.

PROFESSION

He was self-employed and lived off various odd jobs. He sometimes worked in the family pencil factory.

ACTION
Originator of passive resistance, abolitionist

CABIN
Thoreau built his cabin in the forest himself.

TAXES
Thoreau refused to pay his taxes as a form of protest.

PENCIL
He noted everything down in his private diary for over 20 years.

The protestor

Henri Dunant

CONTEXT

The Battle of Solferino took place in Italy on June 24, 1859. It was won by the French and Piedmontese troops, who were fighting the Austrians.

Swiss businessman Henri Dunant was horrified by the carnage at the aftermath of the Battle of Solferino in Italy and organised improvised first aid. This traumatic experience led him to campaign for neutral and proper care for all wounded soldiers. In 1863, he founded the International Committee of the Red Cross with four other Swiss men, and in 1864, he supported the organization of the first Geneva Convention, which laid down the foundations for humanitarian law: neutrality of medical staff, and the obligation to treat all victims.

AWARD

In 1901, Henri Dunant shared the first Nobel Peace Prize with Frédéric Passy, a French pacifist and anticolonialist.

HIS BOOK

In 1862, Henri Dunant published *A Memory of Solferino*. The book, which described the chaos of war and suffering of the soldiers, aroused strong feelings throughout Europe. It allowed Dunant to spread his ideas.

THE SYMBOLS

The International Committee of the Red Cross uses three symbols: the red cross, formed by reversing the colors of the Swiss flag; the red crescent, formed by reversing the colors of the Ottoman Empire flag; and the red crystal, which does not have any special meaning.

IDENTITY

Humanist, businessman

Swiss and later French (1858)

Born on May 8, 1828, in Geneva

Died on October 30, 1910, in Heiden, Switzerland

ACTION
Founder of the Red Cross and the first Geneva Convention

BUSINESS
He was not a terribly successful businessman, experiencing bankruptcy and financial ruin.

BOOK
A Memory of Solferino has been translated from the original French into over 17 languages.

RED CROSS
Symbol of protection for medical staff, ambulances, and hospitals.

The rescuer

Lejzer Ludwik Zamenhof

The young Lejzer Ludwik Zamenhof belonged to a Jewish family and lived in an area on the Russian-Polish border marked by national and racial conflicts. He began to dream of uniting the peoples of the world from a young age. To achieve his dream, he created an international language and, in 1887, published the first textbook to lay down the foundations of Esperanto. In the years that followed, he worked on developing his project by translating a great many classic works and organizing international conventions.

IDENTITY

Linguist, opthalmologist

Polish

Born on December 15, 1859, in Bialystok

Died on April 14, 1917, in Warsaw

EDUCATION

Zamenhof spoke Russian, Polish, German, Hebrew, and Yiddish. He was also familiar with English, French, Italian, Latin, and ancient Greek.

ESPERANTO

Esperanto is a simple and regular language, without exceptions. It is based on 16 fundamental rules: all the letters are pronounced; nouns end in "o" and adjectives in "a"; verbs do not vary in gender or number; and so on.

POSTERITY

In August 1905, Zamenhof presided over the first World Congress of Esperanto, which was held in Boulogne-sur-Mer, France, and attended by 20 countries. Esperanto still exists today in around 120 countries, but is hardly used by the people who live there.

PROFESSION

A deeply humanist man, he worked as a doctor in very poor areas, often refusing payment for his services.

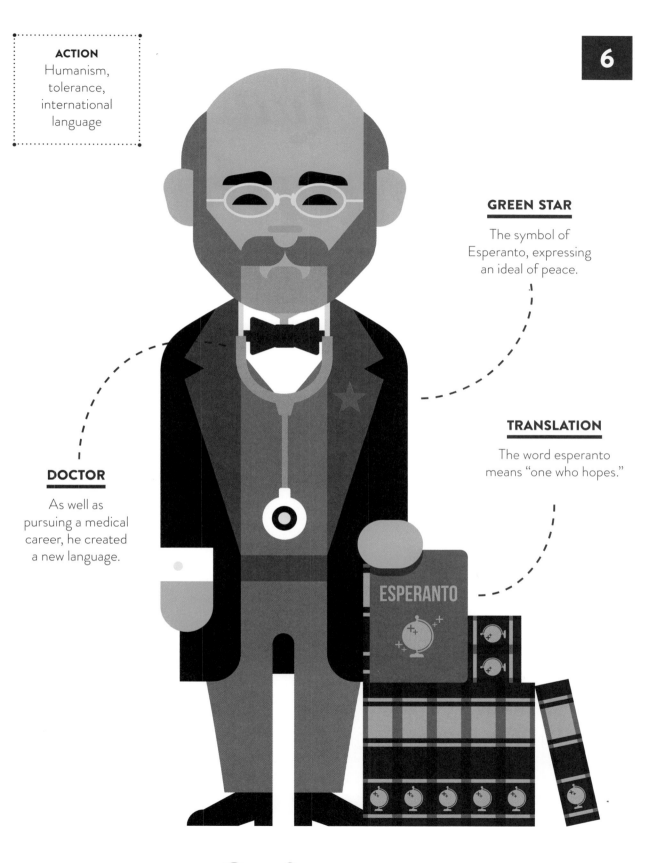

ACTION
Humanism, tolerance, international language

GREEN STAR

The symbol of Esperanto, expressing an ideal of peace.

TRANSLATION

The word esperanto means "one who hopes."

DOCTOR

As well as pursuing a medical career, he created a new language.

ESPERANTO

Dr. Esperanto

Bertha von Suttner

ALLIANCE

Bertha von Suttner was close friends with the wealthy Alfred Nobel, (the inventor of dynamite). It is thought that she encouraged him to create the Nobel Peace Prize.

Endowed with a lively mind and an independent spirit, Bertha von Suttner promoted the cause of pacifism throughout her life. In 1889, she published the novel *Lay Down Your Arms!* It met with great success and she became a leading figure in the pacifist movement. She spoke German, French, Italian, and English fluently, and attended and spoke at countless conferences throughout Europe and the USA. From 1892 to 1914, she was vice president of the International Peace Bureau.

IDENTITY

Peace activist, journalist, writer

Austrian

Born on June 9, 1843, in Prague

Died on June 21, 1914, in Vienna

IPB

Founded in 1891, the International Peace Bureau is the oldest international pacifist organization. It organizes conferences and publishes reports to promote peace.

LAY DOWN YOUR ARMS!

The novel was a bestseller, with its depiction of front-line atrocities as well as daily life in the rear of an army. It tells the story of Martha Althaus, a daughter and wife of military men, who lives through the horrors of four wars, including the 1870 war.

AWARD

The first woman to win the Nobel Peace Prize, awarded in 1905, von Suttner continues to be a highly respected figure today, and her face is depicted on the Austrian two-euro coin.

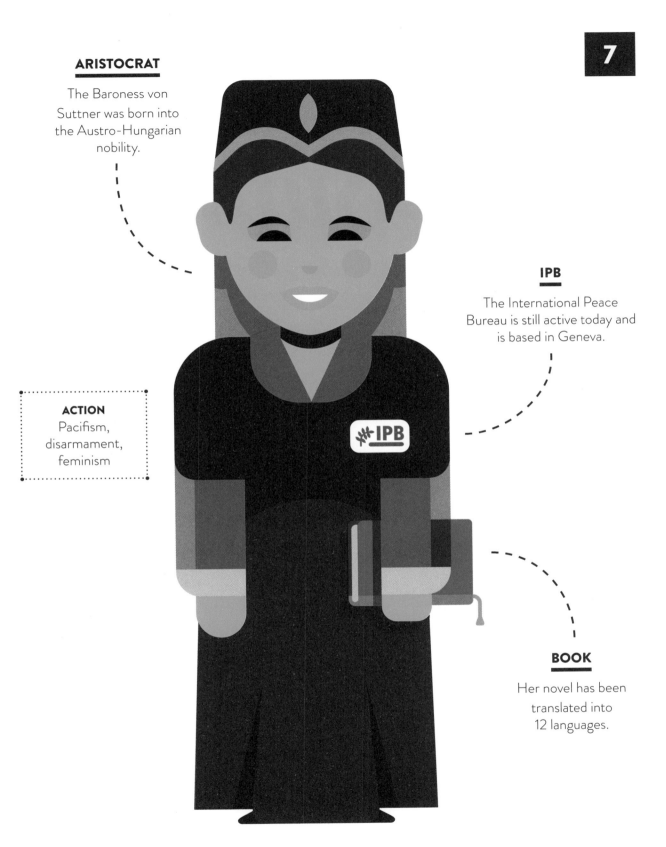

ARISTOCRAT

The Baroness von Suttner was born into the Austro-Hungarian nobility.

IPB

The International Peace Bureau is still active today and is based in Geneva.

ACTION
Pacifism, disarmament, feminism

IPB

BOOK

Her novel has been translated into 12 languages.

The warrior for peace

Jean Jaurès

An **iconic figure and a deputy of French socialism,** Jean Jaurès spent the last years of his life fighting to prevent Europe's descent into war. In 1913, he opposed the Three Year Service Law, in vain. In 1914, he tried to organize a general strike to prevent war, but did not succeed. He was then assassinated by a young nationalist fanatic named Raoul Villain on July 31, 1914, just before the First World War broke out.

EDUCATION

A brilliant student, Jaurès was admitted to the École Normale Supérieure at the top of his class to study philosophy, then came third in the high-level exam for teaching philosophy.

> "The affirmation of peace is the greatest of fights.
>
> Jean Jaurès, 1914

IDENTITY

Politician, teacher, journalist

French

Born on September 3, 1859, in Castres

Assassinated on July 31, 1914, in Paris

Buried in the Panthéon in Paris

HUMANITY

In 1904, Jaurès launched a new newspaper, *L'Humanité*. The daily publication promoted left-wing ideas, particularly the workers' struggle, and the cause of peace. It was socialist to begin with and became communist in 1920.

THE THREE YEAR SERVICE LAW

On May 25, 1913, Jaurès took part in a large pacifist gathering at Pré-Saint-Gervais. He gave a powerful speech opposing the law to extend the length of military service from two to three years.

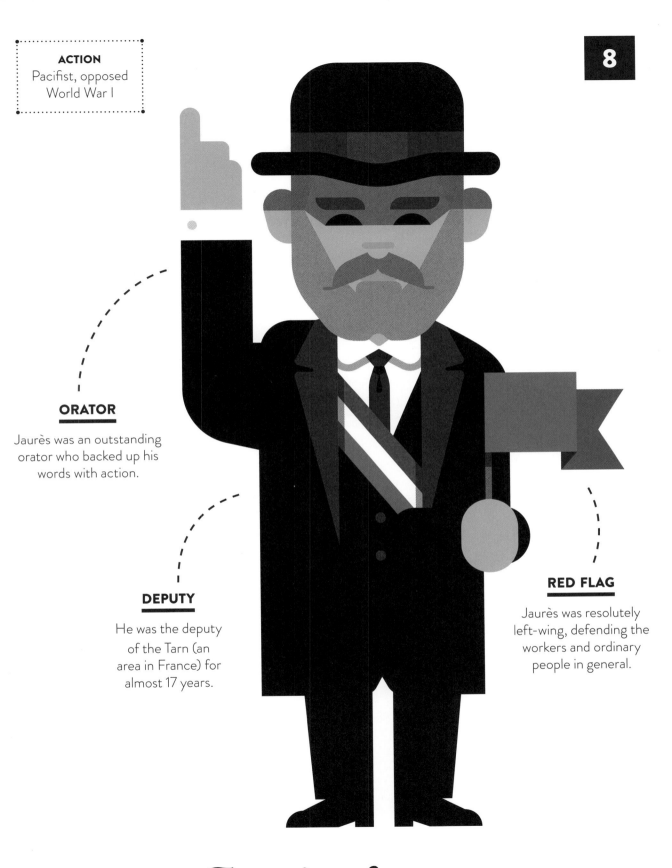

ACTION
Pacifist, opposed
World War I

ORATOR

Jaurès was an outstanding
orator who backed up his
words with action.

DEPUTY

He was the deputy
of the Tarn (an
area in France) for
almost 17 years.

RED FLAG

Jaurès was resolutely
left-wing, defending the
workers and ordinary
people in general.

The voice of peace

Rosa Luxemburg

At the beginning of World War I, German activist Rosa Luxemburg led an anti-war campaign. She was a far-left militant who asked workers not to bear arms and deputies not to vote for war credits (to raise money for war). With her fellow militant, Karl Liebknecht, she founded the Spartacist movement, which supported the 1918 German revolution. But the government violently suppressed the uprising insurrection and had Rosa Luxemburg and Karl Liebknecht assassinated.

IDENTITY

Politician, journalist

Polish, naturalized German

Born on March 5, 1871, in Zamosc

Assassinated on January 15, 1919, in Berlin

REPRESSION

Rosa Luxemburg was imprisoned four times (in 1904, 1906, 1915, and 1916), spending almost four years behind bars.

SPARTACISM

The movement incited workers from every country to refuse to fight each other but instead to fight the capitalist system and its leaders. It takes its name from Spartacus, the slave who rebelled against the Roman Republic.

ON STRIKE

Rosa Luxemburg advocated the idea of a mass strike as the main means of revolutionary action. She disapproved of armed insurrection and declared: "The proletarian revolution has no need of terror to accomplish its goals."

ALLIANCE

In 1916, her comrade Karl Liebknecht was sentenced to hard labor for having shouted "Down with war! Down with the government!"

ACTION
Pacifist, opposed to World War I

NEWSPAPER
She wrote in a newspaper called *Spartacus Letters*.

PRISON
She spent some of the war behind bars.

ON TRIAL
In 1914, she was tried and sentenced for "inciting disobedience against the authorities' law and order."

SPARTACUS

The Revolutionary

Woodrow Wilson

AWARD

Woodrow Wilson received the Nobel Peace Prize in 1919 for his efforts to secure lasting peace after World War I.

The USA entered World War I under his presidency, although he continued to try and find ways to put an end to the conflict. On January 8, 1918, he gave a historic speech, outlining a program based on 14 principles of peace and freedom. The points included the promise of self-determination for all people and the creation of the League of Nations (LN). It was acclaimed by the Europeans but criticized by the US Senate, which rejected the Treaty of Versailles and US membership of the LN!

CONTEXT

On June 28, 1919, the Treaty of Versailles put an end to the war. It was partially based on Wilson's 14 points, including the creation of the LN.

IDENTITY

28th president of the USA

Professor

American

Born on December 28, 1856, in Staunton, VA

Died on February 3, 1924, in Washington, D.C.

FIFTH POINT

In this point, Wilson argued for an impartial arbitration of colonial claims that took into account the interests of the populations concerned. He therefore raised the question of the rights of colonized people, without actually talking about decolonization.

LEAGUE OF NATIONS

This organization, which existed from 1920–1946, had 60 member countries at its peak. It aimed to prevent war, promote disarmament, and work for a universal improvement in people's quality of life. It was the predecessor of the United Nations.

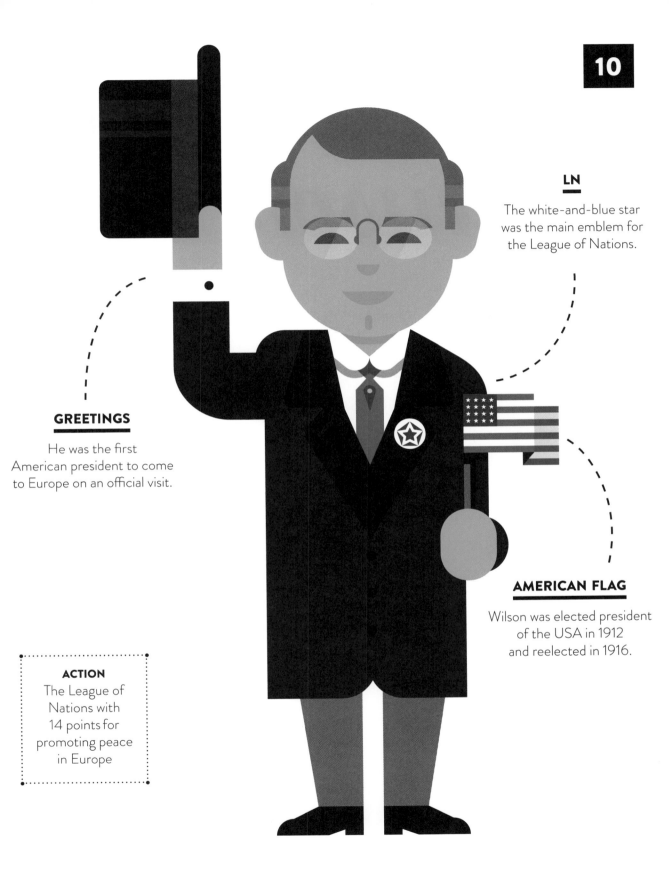

LN

The white-and-blue star was the main emblem for the League of Nations.

GREETINGS

He was the first American president to come to Europe on an official visit.

AMERICAN FLAG

Wilson was elected president of the USA in 1912 and reelected in 1916.

ACTION

The League of Nations with 14 points for promoting peace in Europe

The idealist president

Otto Dix

REPRESSION

Seen as a representative of "degenerate art," Otto Dix was persecuted by the Nazis. His works were banned, or even destroyed.

A former German soldier who fought in World War I, Otto Dix used his art to provide an unflinching account of the horrors of war. In 1924, he produced *The War*, a series of 50 etchings showing the terrible consequences of warfare on people's bodies and minds, with images of dying soldiers, decaying bodies, traumatized civilians, and more. He wanted these shocking images to circulate throughout Germany and encourage people to reject war. But in the end not many people saw them.

WAR WOUNDED

In 1920, Otto Dix painted *The Skat Players,* showing three war veterans with hideously mutilated faces. His paintings *Prague Street* and *The Match Seller* were in the same vein.

IDENTITY

Painter, printmaker

German

Born on December 2, 1891, in Untermhaus

Died on July 25, 1969, in Singen

MACABRE PAINTING

Between 1929 and 1932, Otto Dix painted a triptych called *The War.* It features a faceless army of soldiers on their way to the front, a hellish battlefield strewn with corpses, and a ghostly soldier (possibly himself) returning from the front.

"Abnormal situations bring out all the depravity, the bestiality of human beings."

Otto Dix

PALETTE

A leading figure in the New Objectivity movement, he produced harshly realistic depictions of war.

ACTION
Denunciation of the atrocities of war, antimilitarism

SOLDIER

He volunteered for the army, serving in the artillery and fighting in France and Russia.

WWI

His work bears witness to the brutality of war.

The painter of horror

Aristide Briand

When World War I was over, French statesman Aristide Briand used his energy and his talents as a negotiator to promote a policy of reconciliation with Germany. In 1925, together with German foreign minister Gustav Stresemann he orchestrated the Locarno Treaties and in 1926 he sponsored Germany's entry into the League of Nations (LN). He also wanted to outlaw war, and proposed the Kellogg-Briand Pact with American statesman Frank Kellogg. He was one of the most passionate pacifists of his time.

KELLOGG-BRIAND

The pact was signed on August 27, 1928 in Paris by 63 countries, who promised to use peaceful means to resolve their disputes. Nevertheless, the pact proved powerless to stop World War II a few years later.

LOCARNO

Signed on October 16, 1925, in Locarno, Switzerland, these international treaties guaranteed the borders established after the Great War by the Treaty of Versailles. They also confirmed the demilitarization of the Rhineland.

11

terms as prime minister of France

IDENTITY

Politician, diplomat, lawyer, journalist

French

Born on March 28, 1862, in Nantes

Died on March 7, 1932, in Paris

ACTION
Pacifism, disarmament, Franco-German rapprochement, construction of Europe

FRANCE AND GERMANY

Briand promoted Franco-German reconciliation.

LONG LIFE

He was tireless, staying in power almost until his death.

THE PACT

Germany was a notable signatory of the Kellogg-Briand Pact.

The pilgrim of peace

Erich Maria Remarque

A soldier during World War I, Erich Maria Remarque was conscripted into the German army when he was 18 and sent to the battlefield of Flanders, where he was wounded. He used this terrible experience as the basis for his novel *All Quiet on the Western Front*, which described the horrors of war. Published in 1929, the book was hugely popular, and was even adapted for the cinema in 1930. But the Nazis were not happy with Remarque's antimilitarist message, and he had to go into exile in Switzerland and the USA.

Brilliantly directed by Lewis Milestone, the film was a huge success, winning two Oscars—for best picture and best director.

20
million copies sold, translated into 50 languages

IDENTITY

Born Erich Paul Remark

Writer

German, naturalized American

Born on June 22, 1898, in Osnabrück, Germany

Died on September 25, 1970, in Locarno, Switzerland

NOVEL TITLE

The hero died "on a day that was so quiet and still on the whole front, that the army report confined itself to the single sentence: All quiet on the Western Front." The title uses this final sentence, an ironic reflection on the inhumanity of official war communication.

NAZI FURY

Remarque's pacifism unleashed the fury of the Nazis, who burned the book, banned the film, and stripped the writer of his German nationality in 1938. The Nazis also directed their anger at his sister, Elfriede, and assassinated her in 1943.

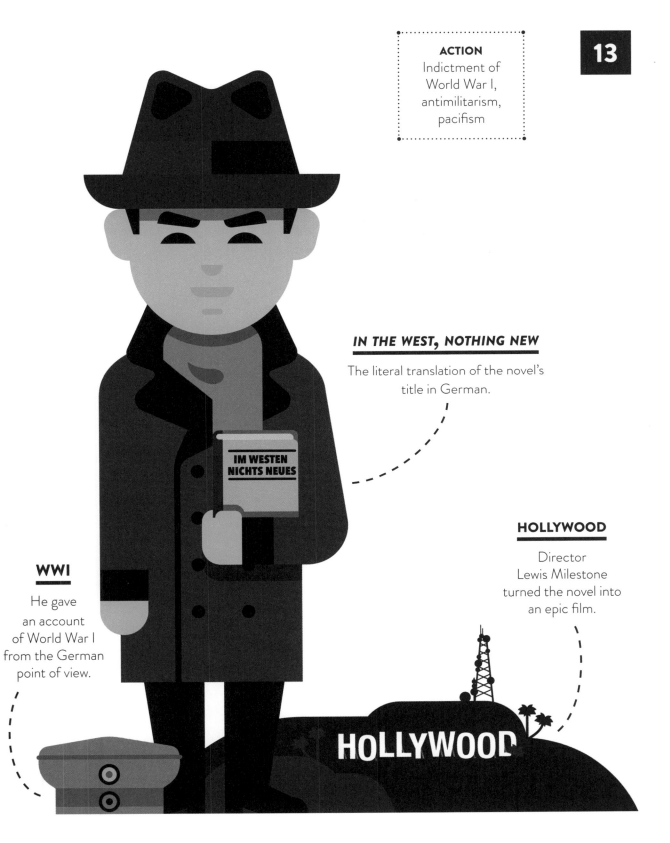

ACTION
Indictment of
World War I,
antimilitarism,
pacifism

IN THE WEST, NOTHING NEW
The literal translation of the novel's
title in German.

IM WESTEN
NICHTS NEUES

HOLLYWOOD
Director
Lewis Milestone
turned the novel into
an epic film.

WWI
He gave
an account
of World War I
from the German
point of view.

HOLLYWOOD

The former soldier

Pablo Picasso

Considered the greatest artist of the 20th century, Pablo Picasso was always willing to put his extraordinary talent to use in promoting peace. In 1937, he painted one of his most famous works, *Guernica*, symbolizing the atrocities of war. In 1949, he created his first dove of peace, for the poster used by the World Congress of Intellectuals in Defense of Peace in Paris. He later drew many other doves, helping to popularize the bird as a universal symbol of peace.

CONTEXT

The World Congress of Intellectuals in Defense of Peace was an international conference held in 1949 to promote peace. It was supported by Picasso.

50,000
works of art created

GUERNICA

This painting is based on an incident during the Spanish Civil War, when the Spanish Basque town of Guernica was bombed by planes sent by the German Nazis and Italian fascists. It depicts violence, suffering, and death.

WAR AND PEACE

In the 1950s, Picasso transformed the Vallauris chapel in the south of France into a temple of peace. He covered the walls with the *War and Peace* murals. One of the main characters in the murals is a peace warrior carrying a shield decorated with a dove.

IDENTITY

Painter, sculptor

Spanish

Born on October 25, 1881, in Malaga, Spain

Died on April 8, 1973, in Mougins, France

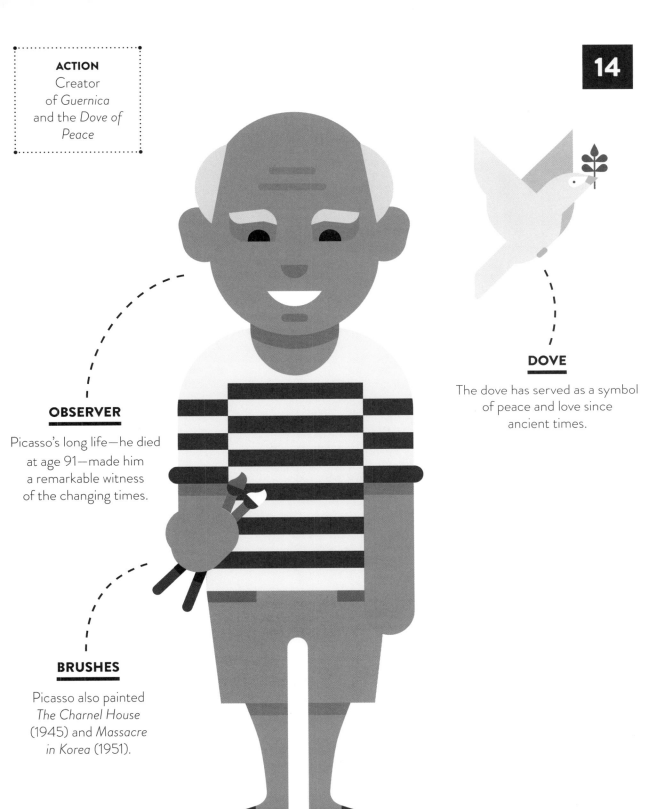

ACTION
Creator
of *Guernica*
and the *Dove of
Peace*

DOVE

The dove has served as a symbol
of peace and love since
ancient times.

OBSERVER

Picasso's long life—he died
at age 91—made him
a remarkable witness
of the changing times.

BRUSHES

Picasso also painted
The Charnel House
(1945) and *Massacre
in Korea* (1951).

The genius artist

Dalton Trumbo

IDENTITY

Writer, director, screenwriter

American

Born on December 9, 1905, in Montrose, CO

Died on September 10, 1976, in Los Angeles, CA

In 1938, when he was starting out as a Hollywood screenwriter, Dalton Trumbo wrote the novel *Johnny Got His Gun.* The book tells the story of the suffering and dreams of a young American soldier who fought in World War I and was horribly mutilated: he is deaf, dumb, and blind and has lost his arms and legs—but his mind still functions. A pacifist with a great love of liberty, Trumbo's book was a harrowing indictment of the absurdity of war.

PROFESSION

A talented screenwriter, Dalton Trumbo worked on many famous films, such as Stanley Kubrick's *Spartacus* (1960) and Otto Preminger's *Exodus* (1960).

WITCH HUNT

In 1947, Dalton Trumbo was accused of communism by the House Un-American Activities Committee. In 1950, he was sentenced to a year in jail and banned from working in Hollywood. He kept on working, using various pseudonyms, until 1960.

THE FILM

Dalton Trumbo adapted his novel for the cinema in 1971. We see Johnny, lying in his hospital bed, recalling the past and reconnecting to the world around him with the only sense he has left: the sensitivity of his skin.

AWARD

The only film that Dalton Trumbo made, *Johnny Got His Gun*, made a lasting impression, winning the Grand Prize of the Jury at the Cannes Film Festival in 1971.

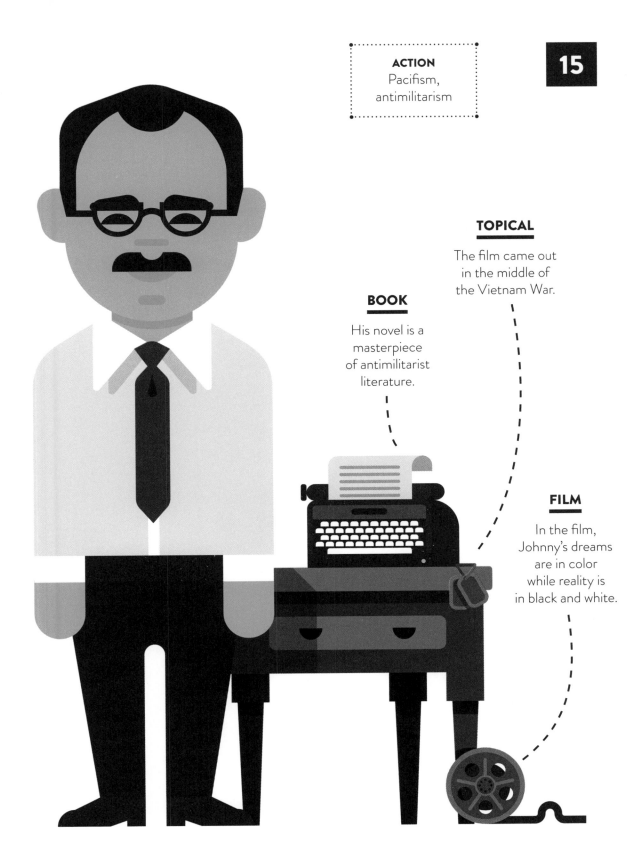

ACTION
Pacifism,
antimilitarism

TOPICAL

The film came out
in the middle of
the Vietnam War.

BOOK

His novel is a
masterpiece
of antimilitarist
literature.

FILM

In the film,
Johnny's dreams
are in color
while reality is
in black and white.

The war critic

Charlie Chaplin

The character he created in 1914, The Tramp, brought Charlie Chaplin worldwide fame. But his status as a huge Hollywood star did not stop him from making politically engaged films. In 1940, he released *The Great Dictator*, a satirical film that made fun of Nazism while underlining how dangerous it was. Chaplin's performance as Hynkel, a character based on Hitler, gave him his greatest triumph and helped to raise the American public's awareness of the tragedy unfolding in Europe.

PROFESSION

Over a period of around 50 years, he made over 80 films, including both silent and talking pictures.

CONTEXT

World War II lasted from 1939 to 1945. The USA entered the war against Germany, Italy, and Japan in 1941.

IDENTITY

Actor, director

British

Born on April 16, 1889, in London, UK

Died on December 25, 1977, in Corsier-sur-Vevey, Switzerland

THE GREAT DICTATOR

Chaplin played two parts: the dictator, Adenoid Hynkel, and his double, the Jewish barber. At the end of the film, the Jewish barber is mistaken for the dictator and spontaneously makes an impassioned speech defending freedom, tolerance, democracy, and peace.

SHOULDER ARMS

In 1918, during World War I, Charlie Chaplin filmed *Shoulder Arms*, a comedy that took a lighthearted look at the daily life of soldiers. A deeply committed pacifist, the actor was already attempting to highlight the absurdity of the war.

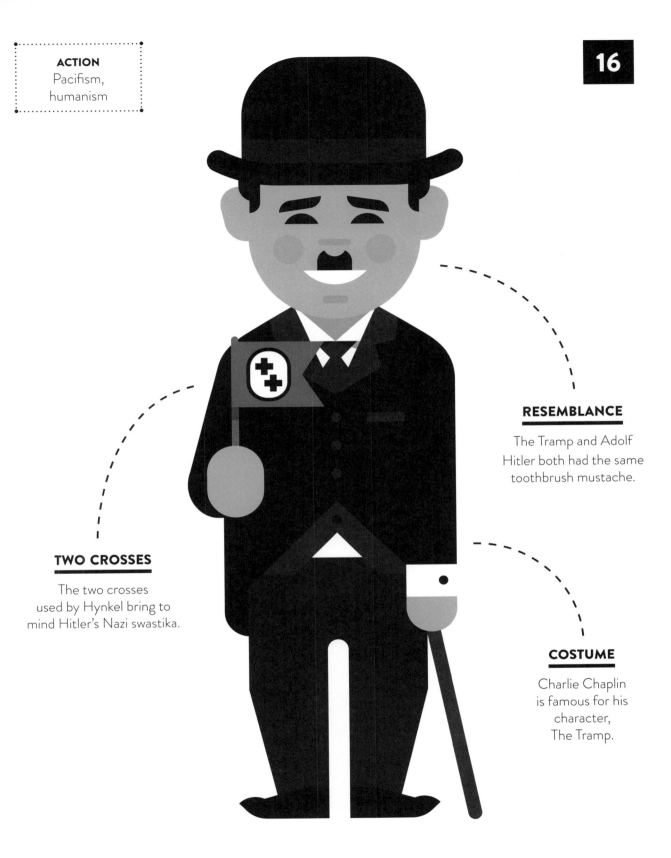

ACTION
Pacifism,
humanism

RESEMBLANCE

The Tramp and Adolf
Hitler both had the same
toothbrush mustache.

TWO CROSSES

The two crosses
used by Hynkel bring to
mind Hitler's Nazi swastika.

COSTUME

Charlie Chaplin
is famous for his
character,
The Tramp.

The film icon

Sophie Scholl

CONTEXT

From 1933 to 1945, Adolf Hitler and his Nazi party imposed a reign of terror on Germany and drew a great many countries into World War II.

During the summer of 1942, a 21-year-old German student, Sophie Scholl, rebelled against the Nazi dictatorship. She joined her brother Hans and other young dissenters who had just founded the underground White Rose group. On February 18, 1943, Sophie and Hans were distributing anti-Nazi leaflets in the University of Munich. They were reported by the caretaker and arrested by the Gestapo. Four days later, they were sentenced to death and executed immediately.

TAKING RISKS

Like her friends, Sophie Scholl took more and more risks. In February 1943, she distributed leaflets in broad daylight in the center of Munich, including in telephone booths and on parked cars.

THE WHITE ROSE

The group wrote pacifist slogans on the walls and composed six leaflets denouncing the Nazis' aggressive and anti-semitic policy. Their last leaflet called on students to rise up and overthrow Hitler's dictatorship.

ALLIANCE

Hans Scholl and Alexander Schmorell were two medical students who founded the White Rose group. Alexander was executed five months after Hans.

IDENTITY

Student

German

Born on May 9, 1921, in Forchtenberg

Died on February 22, 1943, in Munich

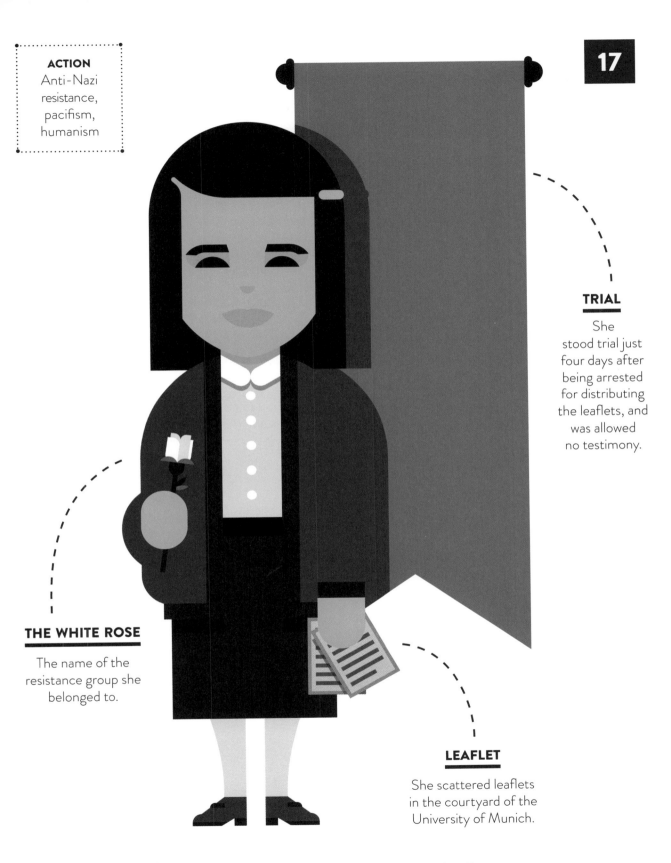

ACTION
Anti-Nazi resistance, pacifism, humanism

17

TRIAL
She stood trial just four days after being arrested for distributing the leaflets, and was allowed no testimony.

THE WHITE ROSE
The name of the resistance group she belonged to.

LEAFLET
She scattered leaflets in the courtyard of the University of Munich.

The resistance activist

Raoul Wallenberg

In 1944, when the Nazis began to exterminate the Jewish in Hungary, the American War Refugee Board recruited Swedish businessman Raoul Wallenberg to aid the Jewish in Budapest. The difficulties and the risks did not stop him taking action over and over again. His main tool was Swedish neutrality: he gave Jewish people Swedish passports and sheltered them in buildings under Swedish protection. Raoul Wallenberg saved the lives of tens of thousands of Jews.

DISAPPEARED

In January 1945, the Soviets liberated Budapest—and arrested Raoul Wallenberg, whom they suspected of being an American spy. After his arrest, all trace of him was lost. Did he die in prison? Was he assassinated? The mystery has never been solved.

IDENTITY

Diplomat, businessman

Swedish

Born on August 4, 1912, in Lidingö

Disappeared

WAR REFUGEE BOARD

In January 1944, American President Franklin D. Roosevelt, set up the War Refugee Board as an agency for helping civilian victims of the Nazi regime. The staff collaborated with Jewish organizations, resistance activitists, and neutral countries.

PROFESSION

In the 1930s, Wallenberg was working for an import-export company. He often visited Budapest, and learned to speak Hungarian.

AWARD

In 1963, Israel awarded Wallenberg the title Righteous Among the Nations, a distinction that honors non-Jews who have helped Jews.

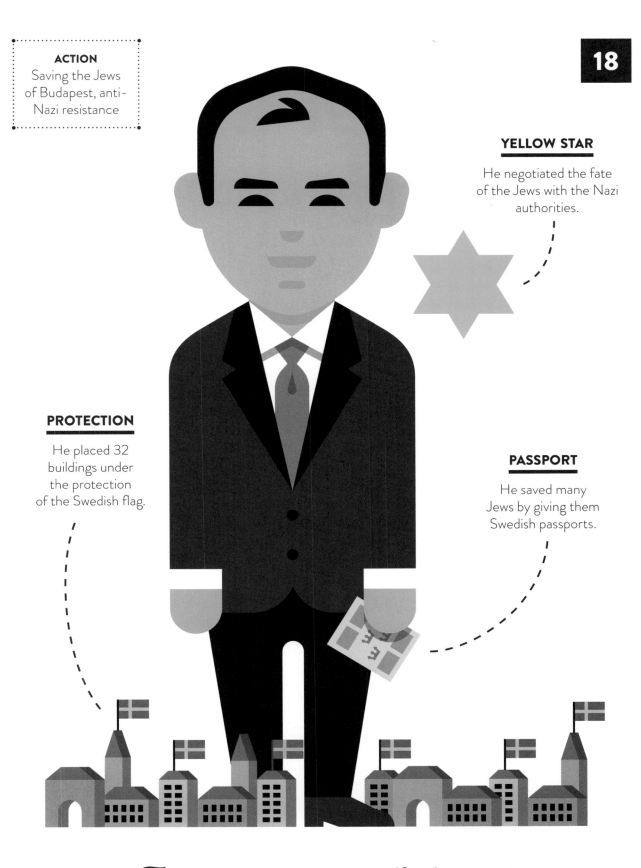

ACTION
Saving the Jews of Budapest, anti-Nazi resistance

YELLOW STAR
He negotiated the fate of the Jews with the Nazi authorities.

PROTECTION
He placed 32 buildings under the protection of the Swedish flag.

PASSPORT
He saved many Jews by giving them Swedish passports.

The courageous diplomat

Albert Einstein

IDENTITY

Scientist, physicist

German, naturalized Swiss and American

Born on March 14, 1879, in Ulm, Germany

Died on April 18, 1955, in Princeton, NJ, USA

Because he was concerned about the dangerous proliferation of nuclear weapons, the physicist Albert Einstein used his worldwide fame to champion peace. He spent the last ten years of his life speaking at conferences and on the radio, and writing articles for the press. In 1946, he founded and became chairman of the Emergency Committee of Atomic Scientists, and in 1955 he signed the Russell-Einstein manifesto, which called on world leaders to settle their conflicts peacefully.

ALLIANCE

The British mathematician and philosopher Bertrand Russell was fiercely opposed to the use of nuclear energy in weapons.

MISTAKEN

Fearing that Nazi Germany would win the nuclear arms race, Einstein encouraged the USA to step up its research program. The USA went on to develop the first atomic bomb and dropped it on Hiroshima, which greatly distressed the pacifist Einstein.

$E=MC^2$

In 1905, Einstein produced the famous equation $E=mc^2$, which establishes an equivalence between mass and energy. But he did not contribute directly to research on nuclear physics and its military applications that use this equation.

> "The fate of humanity is entirely dependent upon its moral development."
>
> Albert Einstein

ACTION
Pacifism, nuclear disarmament, antimilitarism

GENIUS
A brilliant physicist, he received the Nobel Prize in Physics in 1921.

GRIMACE
He stuck out his tongue in a famous photograph from 1951, an image that symbolizes his free spirit.

ATOMIC WEAPONS
A deeply committed pacifist, he opposed nuclear weapons.

The 20th-century genius

Mahatma Gandhi

Mohandas Gandhi appeared on the Indian political scene around 1917. He called for the independence of India, which was then still part of the British Empire, but resolved to use only peaceful means to attain it: he recommended boycotting British products and refusing to pay taxes as well as organizing strikes, rallies, marches, and hunger strikes. The British government finally gave in and proclaimed Indian independence in 1947, but the country was then hit by a wave of terrible violence and Gandhi was assassinated in 1948.

IDENTITY

Lawyer, politician, activist

Indian

Born on October 2, 1869 in Porbandar State, Kathiawar Agency, British Indian Empire (now in Gujarat, India)

Died on January 30, 1948 New Delhi, India

CONTEXT

Independence led to the partition of Indian territory into two separate states: India, mainly Hindu; and Pakistan, mostly Muslim.

HUNGER STRIKE

Gandhi, a Hindu, did everything he could to reconcile the Hindu and Muslim communities. Toward the end of his life, at the age of 78, he continued not eating and put his health at risk to exert pressure on public opinion.

A GREAT SOUL

Gandhi championed all oppressed people, including women and the "untouchables," who were judged by Indians to be impure and who were rejected by traditional Hindu society. He was a strict vegetarian and was opposed to animal sacrifices.

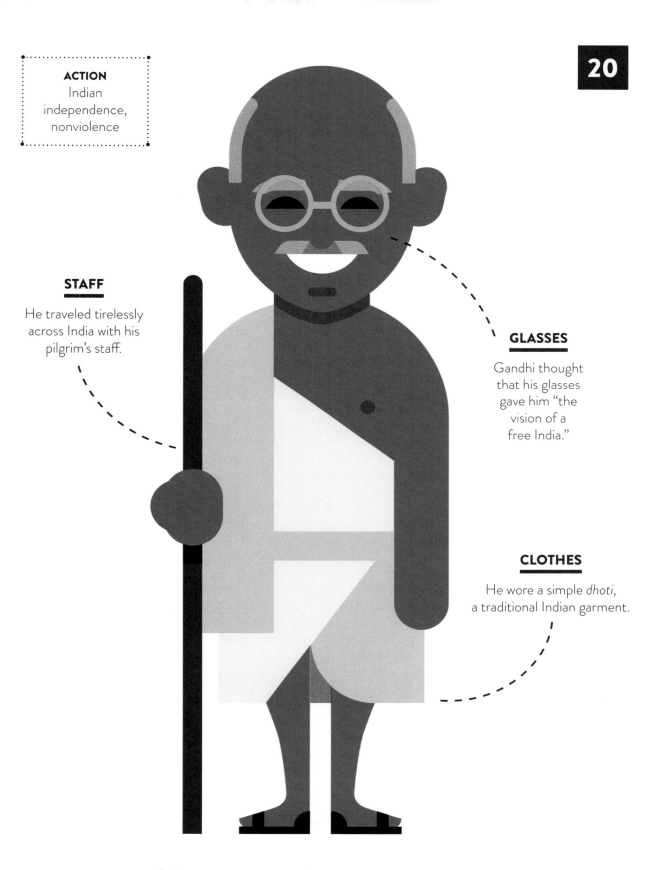

ACTION
Indian independence, nonviolence

STAFF
He traveled tirelessly across India with his pilgrim's staff.

GLASSES
Gandhi thought that his glasses gave him "the vision of a free India."

CLOTHES
He wore a simple *dhoti*, a traditional Indian garment.

The soul of nonviolence

Eleanor Roosevelt

The wife of American president Franklin D. Roosevelt, Eleanor Roosevelt took her role as first lady very seriously. She was particularly active in defending women's rights and denouncing racial segregation. When her husband died, she continued her work at the UN. She was the chair of the United Nations Commission on Human Rights from 1946 to 1951, and played a key role in the drawing up and ratification of the Universal Declaration of Human Rights (UDHR) in 1948.

CONTEXT

Eleanor Roosevelt was the niece of Theodore Roosevelt, president from 1901 to 1909, and the wife of Franklin D. Roosevelt, president from 1933 to 1945.

IDENTITY

First lady of the USA

American

Born on October 11, 1884, in New York

Died on November 7, 1962, in New York

FEMINIST

Eleanor Roosevelt began to campaign for improving women's living conditions in the 1920s. At the White House, she even went as far as holding a weekly press conference for women journalists only!

THE UDHR

Adopted on December 10, 1948, the Universal Declaration of Human Rights sets out the civil, political, and social rights of all human beings, without distinction of any kind, such as race, sex, religion, or nationality.

ALLIANCE

The UDHR was drawn up by nine experts from all regions of the world, including eminent French jurist René Cassin, who drafted most of the text.

21

ACTION
Human rights, feminism, opposed racial segregation

SOCIETY WOMAN
Eleanor Roosevelt was born into a wealthy New York family.

UNITED NATIONS
Emblem of the UN (United Nations)

THE UDHR
It is made up of an introduction and 30 articles.

The stateswoman

Martin Luther King

Reverend Martin Luther King was one of the main leaders of the African American civil rights movement, which demanded the right to vote and fought racial oppression. In 1955, he organized the Montgomery bus boycott, and in 1963 he was one of the leaders of the peaceful March on Washington for Jobs and Freedom. His nonviolent actions met with success, leading to the passing of progressive laws in 1964 and 1965 that abolished the principles of racial discrimination.

IDENTITY

Baptist minister

American

Born on January 15, 1929, in Atlanta, GA

Assassinated on April 4, 1968, in Memphis, TN

REPRESSION

Although he was totally committed to nonviolence, Martin Luther King was subjected to arrests, threats, and attacks. He was assassinated at the age of 39.

THE BUS BOYCOTT

The conflict began with the arrest of Rosa Parks, a black woman who refused to give up her place on a bus to a white man. It lasted over a year and ended in victory for Parks and King: segregation was banned from all public buses.

"I HAVE A DREAM"

The March on Washington took place on August 28, 1963, and ended with Martin Luther King's famous speech: "I Have a Dream." In it, he expressed his hope for a united, fraternal America where everyone's rights would be respected.

AWARD

King reached the height of his popularity in 1964, when he received the Nobel Peace Prize at age 35.

22

SPEECH

He is seen as one of the greatest orators of the 20th century.

MEDIA

"I Have a Dream" was broadcast live on television.

LINCOLN MEMORIAL

He spoke in front of the Lincoln Memorial, a reminder of the abolition of slavery.

ACTION

Civil rights in the USA, nonviolence

The civil rights champion

Joan Baez

ALLIANCE

Joan Baez is very good friends with Bob Dylan, another politically engaged singer and author of the peace anthem "Blowin' in the Wind."

An American singer, songwriter, and composer, Baez's music has always been inextricably linked to her political convictions and the defense of peace, freedom, and social justice. She supported the civil rights movement and took part in the 1963 March on Washington alongside Martin Luther King. She campaigned against the Vietnam War, and in 1972 went to Hanoi, the capital of North Vietnam, which had been bombed by the Americans. She has continued to champion human rights ever since.

AWARD

Joan Baez received the Ambassador of Conscience Award from Amnesty International in 2015 for having used her talents to promote human rights.

VIETNAM

Joan Baez's visit to Vietnam left a lasting impression on her. In 1973, she released the album *Where Are You Now, My Son?* The B-side featured a recording lasting around 20 minutes with a mixture of songs, speeches, air raid sirens, and the noise of bombing.

HIT SONG

"Here's to You" is one of Joan Baez's best known songs. She pays homage to Sacco and Vanzetti, two Italian immigrant anarchists sentenced to death for robbery and executed in 1927, despite serious doubts over whether they were guilty.

IDENTITY

Folk music singer, politically engaged artist

American

Born on January 9, 1941, in New York

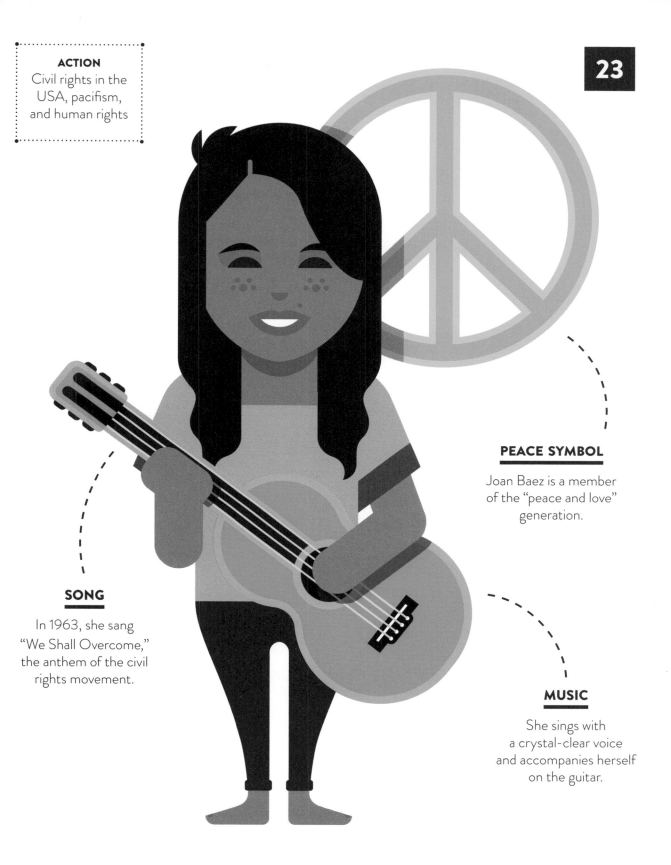

23

ACTION
Civil rights in the USA, pacifism, and human rights

PEACE SYMBOL
Joan Baez is a member of the "peace and love" generation.

SONG
In 1963, she sang "We Shall Overcome," the anthem of the civil rights movement.

MUSIC
She sings with a crystal-clear voice and accompanies herself on the guitar.

The queen of folk

Muhammad Ali

Ali won the world heavyweight boxing title three times: in 1964 against Liston; in 1974 against Foreman; and in 1978 against Spinks.

Olympic and world boxing champion, the American Muhammad Ali was 25 when he refused to do his military service and go and fight in Vietnam. In 1967, the American courts sentenced him to a $10,000 fine and five years in prison. He was also stripped of his world title and banned from boxing. But Muhammad Ali did not give in and appealed against the decision. He avoided jail and got his license back in 1970. He returned to the ring and became world champion once again.

ANTI-WAR

Muhammad Ali declared that he was a conscientious objector and refused to fight in a war that went against his religious and moral beliefs. He justified his position, saying, "I ain't got no quarrel with the Viet Cong."

IDENTITY

Boxer

American

Born on January 17, 1942, in Louisville, KY

Died on June 3, 2016, in Scottsdale, AZ

CONTEXT

Muhammad Ali defended the rights of African Americans and human rights in general. He was appointed a UN Messenger of Peace from 1998 to 2008.

NAME

Born Cassius Clay, he abandoned a name rooted in slavery and changed it to Muhammad Ali in 1964. This was a religious and political act that went hand in hand with his conversion to Islam, as part of the African American Nation of Islam movement.

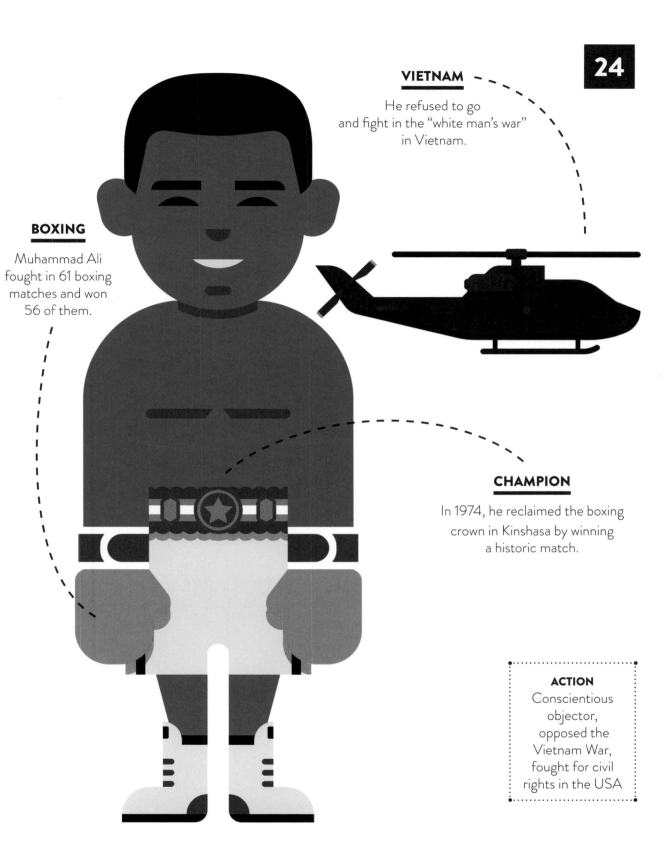

24

VIETNAM

He refused to go
and fight in the "white man's war"
in Vietnam.

BOXING

Muhammad Ali
fought in 61 boxing
matches and won
56 of them.

CHAMPION

In 1974, he reclaimed the boxing
crown in Kinshasa by winning
a historic match.

ACTION
Conscientious
objector,
opposed the
Vietnam War,
fought for civil
rights in the USA

The world champion

John Lennon

IDENTITY

Singer, songwriter, composer

British

Born on October 9, 1940, in Liverpool, UK

Assassinated on December 8, 1980, in New York

In the 1960s, John Lennon was a member of the Beatles, a British pop and rock band that achieved worldwide fame. He then embarked on a solo career and used his huge popularity to promote the cause of peace. In 1969, John Lennon and Yoko Ono took advantage of the world's interest in their marriage to denounce the Vietnam War and promote world peace. In Amsterdam and Montreal, they organized "bed-ins" where, sitting in their wedding bed, they received friends and journalists to talk about peace and love.

PROFESSION

The Beatles were made up of Paul McCartney, George Harrison, Ringo Starr, and John Lennon. They sold over a billion records!

"IMAGINE"

In 1971, Lennon relayed another peace message with his famous song "Imagine." He sang: "Imagine there's no countries, it isn't hard to do, nothing to kill or die for, and no religion too."

GIVE PEACE A CHANCE

A powerful peace anthem, the song "Imagine" was recorded June 1, 1969, in a suite of the Queen Elizabeth hotel during the Montreal bed-in. Sitting in his bed, John Lennon sang and played the guitar, while everyone who was there joined in.

AWARD

In 1969, he returned his Member of the Order of the British Empire medal to denounce the country's involvement in the Biafran and Vietnam wars.

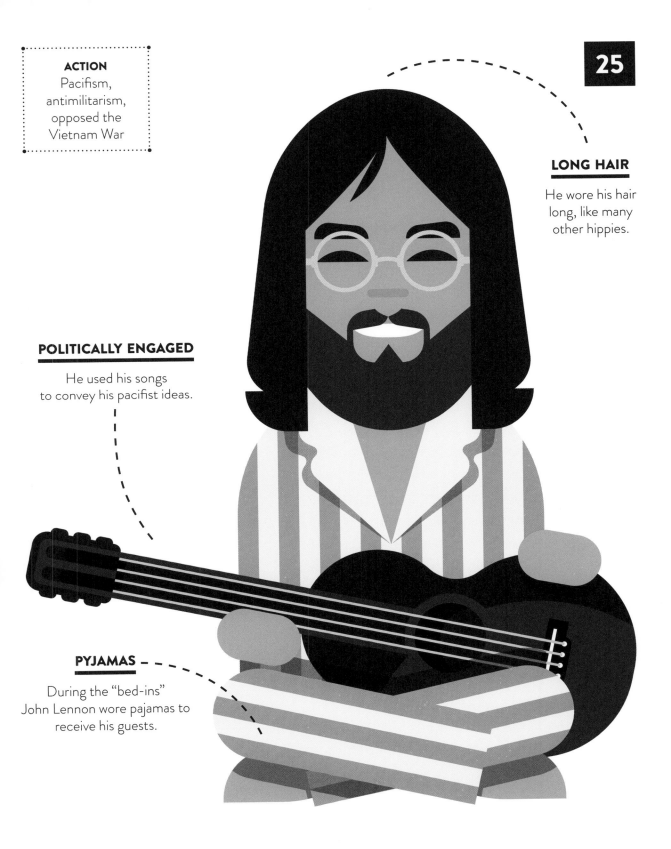

25

ACTION
Pacifism, antimilitarism, opposed the Vietnam War

LONG HAIR
He wore his hair long, like many other hippies.

POLITICALLY ENGAGED
He used his songs to convey his pacifist ideas.

PYJAMAS
During the "bed-ins" John Lennon wore pajamas to receive his guests.

The activist pop star

Adolfo Pérez Esquivel

AWARD

He received the Nobel Peace Prize in 1980, and has continued to campaign in Latin America and take part in humanitarian missions around the world.

Adolfo Pérez Esquivel is an Argentinian artist and art teacher who defends human rights in Latin America. In 1973, he founded the newspaper *Peace and Justice* to convey his ideas, and in 1974 he cofounded the Service, Peace, and Justice Foundation (SERPAJ), which uses nonviolent means to fight against the oppression of Latin American people. He has been jailed for his activities, but continues to resist and campaign peacefully, particularly in support of children, indigenous people, and nature.

REPRESSION

In 1977, he was arrested by the military junta and spent 14 months in prison. He is a fervent Catholic and says that he survived thanks to his faith.

DICTATORSHIP

Military juntas ruled most Latin American countries in the 1970s and 1980s. In Argentina, a violent dictatorship held power from 1976 to 1983. Under its rule, thousands of people were jailed as political prisoners, killed, or made to disappear.

SERPAJ

SERPAJ operates in 13 countries and works on changing attitudes. Its goal is to develop a culture of peace in order to wipe out all forms of violence: within couples, at work, in society, and at the highest levels of the state.

IDENTITY

Activist, fine artist, writer

Argentinian

Born on November 26, 1931, in Buenos Aires

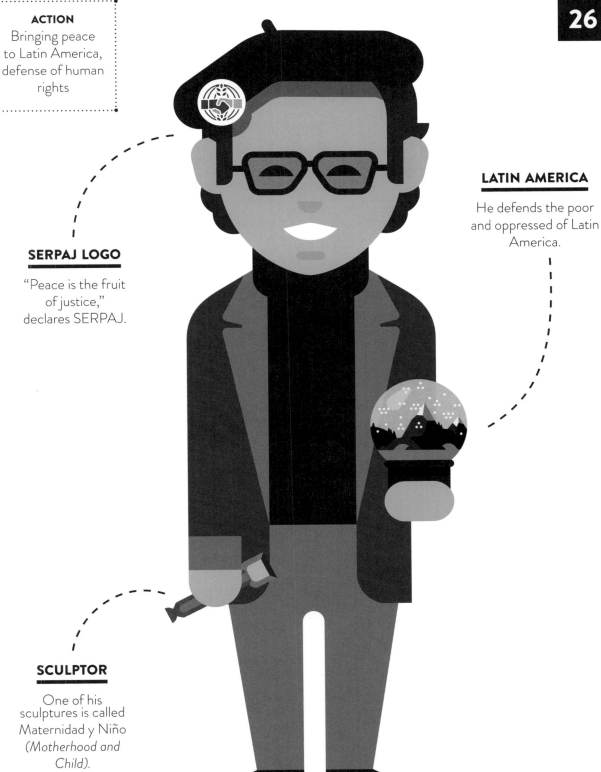

26

ACTION
Bringing peace to Latin America, defense of human rights

SERPAJ LOGO
"Peace is the fruit of justice," declares SERPAJ.

LATIN AMERICA
He defends the poor and oppressed of Latin America.

SCULPTOR
One of his sculptures is called Maternidad y Niño *(Motherhood and Child)*.

The artist activist

M. Corrigan
B. Williams

Fierce hostility between unionists and nationalists plunged Northern Ireland into a cycle of bloodshed that began in 1969. On August 10, 1976, during an armed encounter, a car ran over and killed three of Mairead Corrigan's nephews, a tragedy witnessed by Betty Williams. The two women went on to found Women for Peace (later renamed Peace People), a pacifist movement that sought to reconcile the two communities. Despite their efforts, the conflict continued until the Good Friday Agreement in 1998.

CONTEXT

The Northern Irish conflict pitted Unionists (mostly Protestant), who wanted to remain within the United Kingdom against nationalists (mostly Catholic), who campaigned for independence.

IDENTITY

Pacifists

Northern Irish

Mairead Corrigan born on January 27, 1944, in Belfast

Betty Williams born on May 22, 1943, in Belfast

THEIR MOVEMENT

The Women for Peace movement organized several nonviolent demonstrations in the streets of Belfast, bringing together tens of thousands of people, Catholics and Protestants alike.

THE PEACE WALLS

The "peace walls" (or rather, walls of shame) started to go up in 1969 in the heart of Belfast, separating the Catholic and Protestant districts. In 2013, the government pledged to destroy them by 2023.

AWARD

Mairead Corrigan and Betty Williams were jointly award the Nobel Peace Prize in 1976. They are also members of the pacifist foundation PeaceJam.

27

MAIREAD CORRIGAN
She comes from a Catholic family.

BETTY WILLIAMS
Her father was Protestant and her mother Catholic.

ACTION
End of the Northern Irish conflict, pacifism, nonviolence

PEACE WALL
They want to pull down the walls that divided the Northern Irish people.

The Northern Irish friends

Wangari Maathai

IDENTITY

Biologist, environmental activist

Kenyan

Born on April 1, 1940, in Ihithe

Died on September 25, 2011, in Nairobi

The Kenyan environmental activist Wangari Maathai founded the Green Belt Movement in 1977 to encourage women to plant trees. Her program had two main goals: combating deforestation and soil erosion on the one hand, and, on the other hand, helping women by restoring their main source of fuel and providing them with improved soil, work, and respect. More broadly, Wangari Maathai felt that by improving the environment, she was creating a system that would encourage progress and peace.

AWARD

Wangari Maathai was the first African woman to receive the Nobel Peace Prize. She was awarded the prize in 2004 for her nonviolent actions to protect the environment.

> "When we plant trees, we plant the seeds of peace and seeds of hope."
>
> Wangari Maathai

DEMOCRAT

Wangari Maathai fought for democracy under the authoritarian regime of President Arap Moi. She called for open elections and an end to corruption. Her political activism landed her in jail several times.

GIFTED

Wangari Maathai was a brilliant student who studied biology and veterinary medicine. She then worked as a researcher and a professor at the University of Nairobi. In 1971, she became the first woman in East and Central Africa to earn a doctorate degree.

28

KENYAN FLAG

She entered the Kenyan parliament in 2002 and the government in 2003.

TRADITIONAL COSTUME

She belonged to the Kikuyu, the biggest ethnic group in Kenya.

TREE

Her foundation has planted over 51 million trees in Kenya.

ACTION
Environment, sustainable development, women's rights, democracy

The mother of trees

Ikuo Hirayama

ALLIANCE

Nominated as a UNESCO goodwill ambassador in 1989, he used his talent and charisma to promote culture and peace.

On August 6, 1945, an American atomic bomb was dropped on the Japanese city of Hiroshima and killed over 90,000 people. The survivors included a 15-year-old boy: Ikuo Hirayama. He grew up to become a renowned artist and painted *The Holocaust of Hiroshima*, a huge bloodred work that represents the tragic attack. He was also committed to protecting the world's cultural heritage, convinced that these "treasures of humanity" encourage mutual understanding and peace.

CONTEXT

In 1945, the USA used nuclear weapons for the first time. The Americans bombed two Japanese cities: Hiroshima and Nagasaki.

IDENTITY

Painter in the Nihonga school

Japanese

Born on June 15, 1930, in Setoda, Hiroshima Prefecture

Died on December 2, 2009, in Tokyo

SILK ROAD

Ikuo Hirayama converted to Buddhism after the disaster, and his works are permeated with Buddhist spirituality. He also liked to paint the silk road, since he considered it to be a powerful cultural link between the East and the West.

MASTERPIECE

Painted in 1979, *The Holocaust of Hiroshima* depicts the city in the furnace of the nuclear explosion. Because it denounces the horrors of war, Ikuo Hirayama's painting is often compared to Pablo Picasso's *Guernica*.

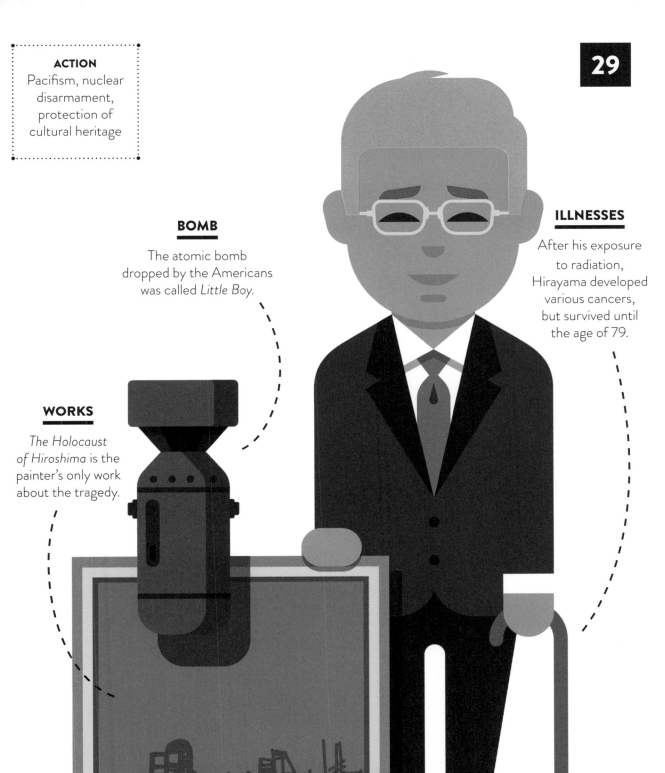

29

ACTION
Pacifism, nuclear disarmament, protection of cultural heritage

BOMB
The atomic bomb dropped by the Americans was called *Little Boy*.

ILLNESSES
After his exposure to radiation, Hirayama developed various cancers, but survived until the age of 79.

WORKS
The Holocaust of Hiroshima is the painter's only work about the tragedy.

The survivor

Tenzin Gyatso

IDENTITY

Buddhist monk

Tibetan (in exile)

Born on July 6, 1935, in Taktser

Tenzin Gyatso, the 14th Dalai Lama, was 15 years old in 1950 when the brand-new People's Republic of China invaded Tibet. Nine years later, he fled occupied Tibet and went into exile in India. Since then, he has dedicated his life to finding a nonviolent solution to the "Tibetan question." He has appealed to the UN for support and travels the world to rally different countries to his cause. His efforts have won him plenty of support and great popularity—but have not helped him to influence Chinese policy.

PEACE PLAN

His five-point peace plan called for: the transformation of the whole of Tibet into a zone of peace; a halt to Chinese immigration; respect for the Tibetan people's fundamental human rights; protection of Tibet's natural environment; and the start of negotiations on the future status of Tibet.

DALAI LAMA

This title, often translated as "Ocean of Wisdom," is given to the great master of Gelugpa, a school of Tibetan Buddhism. In the 17th century, the Dalai Lama also became the spiritual guide and political leader of Tibet.

> "Inner disarmament, external disarmament; these must go together."
>
> Tenzin Gyatso

AWARD

He received the Nobel Peace Prize in 1989 for his nonviolent approach to the Sino-Tibetan conflict and his search for peaceful solutions based on mutual respect.

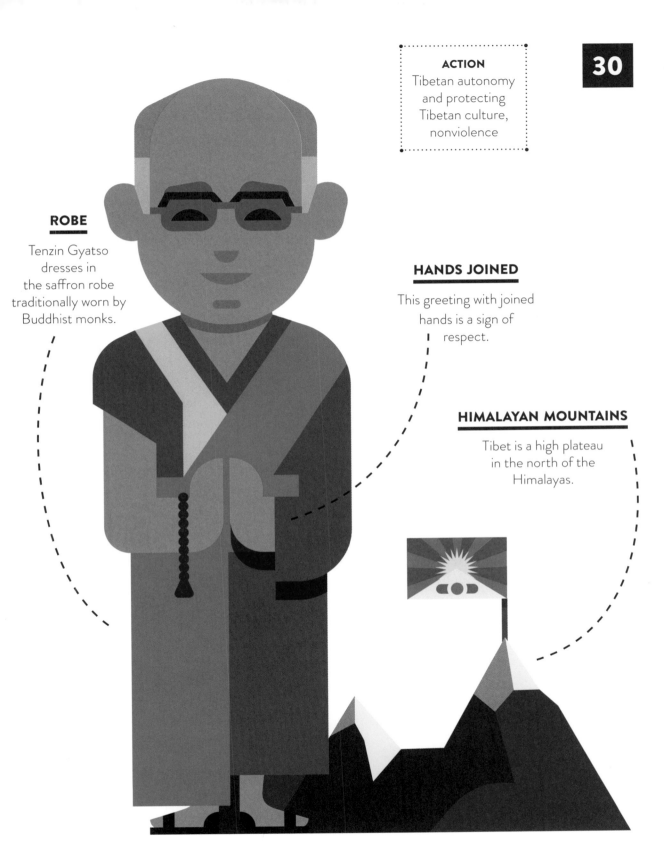

30

ACTION
Tibetan autonomy and protecting Tibetan culture, nonviolence

ROBE

Tenzin Gyatso dresses in the saffron robe traditionally worn by Buddhist monks.

HANDS JOINED

This greeting with joined hands is a sign of respect.

HIMALAYAN MOUNTAINS

Tibet is a high plateau in the north of the Himalayas.

The Dalai Lama

Mikhail Gorbachev

The last leader of the USSR, Mikhail Gorbachev introduced a wave of reform. Domestically, he adopted measures for liberalizing the political landscape and the economy. Internationally, he wanted reconciliation: he reestablished dialogue with the USA and signed disarmament agreements, withdrew from the Afghan conflict, and agreed to the fall of the Berlin wall, resulting in the reunification of Germany and dissolution of the Soviet Bloc. Mikhail Gorbachev played an important part in ending the Cold War.

IDENTITY

Last leader of the USSR (1985–1991)

Soviet/Russian

Born on March 2, 1931, in Privolnoye

CONTEXT

Formed in 1922, the USSR was made up of 15 countries, including Russia. It was dissolved in 1991, following the collapse of the Soviet Bloc.

COLD WAR

From 1947 to 1991, the world was divided into two opposing blocs: the West (the USA and its allies) and the East (the USSR and its allies). This period of hostility was called the Cold War: a conflict that was ideological, diplomatic, and economic rather than military.

DISARMAMENT

Wishing to stop the arms race between the USSR and the USA, Mikhail Gorbachev signed two treaties with Ronald Reagan (in 1987) and George Bush (in 1991), designed to limit short- and medium-range missiles and nuclear weapons.

AWARD

He received the Nobel Peace Prize in 1990 for his nonviolent management of the Cold War and democratic revolutions in eastern Europe.

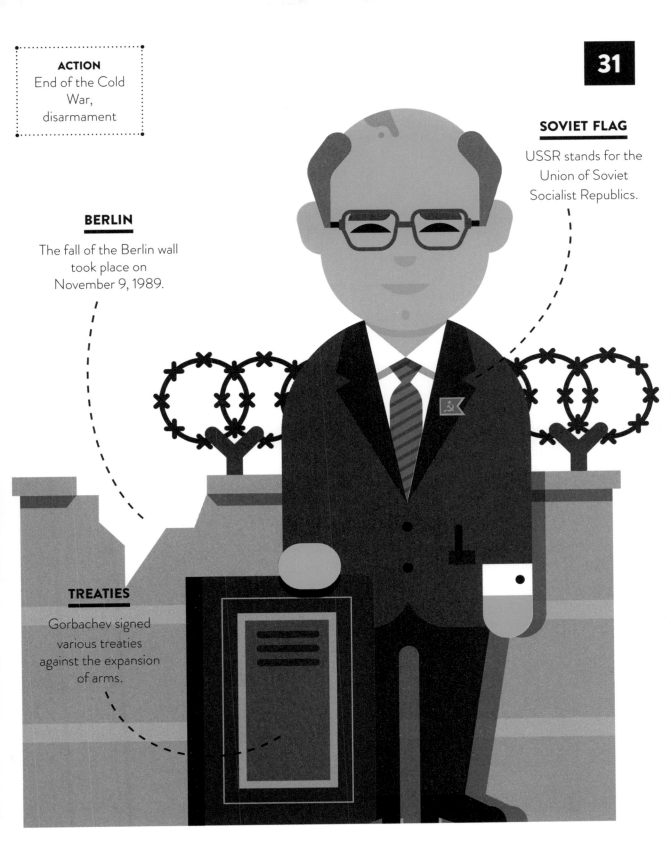

31

ACTION
End of the Cold War, disarmament

SOVIET FLAG
USSR stands for the Union of Soviet Socialist Republics.

BERLIN
The fall of the Berlin wall took place on November 9, 1989.

TREATIES
Gorbachev signed various treaties against the expansion of arms.

The reformer

Václav Havel

CONTEXT

In late 1989, a popular and democratic movement called the Velvet Revolution peacefully freed Czechoslovakia from Soviet control.

A dissident intellectual, Václav Havel denounced the communist regime that was muzzling Czechoslovakia. In 1977, he cofounded the Charter 77 movement, which defended human rights. His ideas landed him in jail more than once, but he did not give up and became very popular. In the autumn of 1989, he led the Velvet Revolution and on December 29, 1989, was elected president. He stayed in power for 13 years, succeeding in obtaining the withdrawal of Soviet troops and democratizing Czechoslovakian institutions.

PLAYWRIGHT

A talented author, Václav Havel wrote around 20 plays. The most famous are *Audience*, *Unveiling*, and *Protest*: satires of a Czechoslovakian society that was being smothered by the communist authorities.

IDENTITY

President of Czechoslovakia, then the Czech Republic

Playwright, intellectual

Czech

Born on October 5, 1936, in Prague

Died on December 18, 2011, in Hrádeček

CHARTER 77

Published on January 1, 1977, Charter 77 was a petition urging the Czechoslovakian government to respect human rights. It was signed by a variety of people, including academics, artists, journalists, and politicians.

REPRESSION

As a political dissident, Václav Havel was thrown into prison several times, and between 1977 and 1989, he spent a total of almost five years behind bars.

ELECTED TO OFFICE

Václav Havel served as president from 1989 to 1992, then from 1993 to 2003.

CHARTER

He was one of the authors and signatories of Charter 77.

THEATER

He wrote plays as well as poems and essays.

The philosopher president

Nelson Mandela

IDENTITY

Referred to by his clan name, Madiba

President of the Republic of South Africa

Political activist, lawyer

South African

Born on July 18, 1918, in Mvezo

Died on December 5, 2013, in Johannesburg

As a committed anti-apartheid activist, Nelson Mandela fought the oppression of the black majority by the white minority in South Africa. His resolute struggles landed him in prison, where he spent 27 years before being released in 1990. He immediately returned to public life and negotiated the abolition of apartheid in 1991. He was extremely popular and elected president of South Africa in 1994. He focused on reconciling the different groups that make up the South African people.

AWARD

Nelson Mandela and President Frederik De Klerk were jointly awarded the Nobel Peace Prize in 1993 for their efforts in establishing democracy.

APARTHEID

Introduced in 1948, the apartheid system was the result of a long tradition of racism in South Africa. It legalized separation between blacks and whites, banning mixed marriages and creating segregated neighborhoods among other measures.

ANC

Nelson Mandela was the leader of the ANC (African National Congress). The anti-apartheid party was nonviolent to begin with, but switched to armed struggle between 1960 and 1990. It then returned to peaceful means and came to power with Mandela.

REPRESSION

Imprisoned from 1962 to 1990, Mandela is the world's most famous political prisoner. International pressure played a large part in his release.

RAISED FIST
A symbol of struggle, strength, and solidarity

FLAG
The flag of South Africa, the rainbow nation.

CHAIN
He was sentenced to imprisonment with hard labor on Robben Island.

ACTION
Fought apartheid in South Africa

The South African legend

Rigoberta Menchú

IDENTITY

Indian rights activist

Guatemalan

Born on January 9, 1959, in Chimel

Rigoberta Menchú is a Guatemalan citizen and member of the K'iche' Maya indigenous people. She rose to prominence in 1983 as she told the story of the suffering of her people, who had been exploited and persecuted by big landowners and the country's military junta. Emerging as the spokesperson for Guatemala's indigenous peoples, she ceaselessly denounced the dictatorship until it was abolished in 1996, before joining efforts to rebuild Guatemala, emphasizing social justice and ethno-cultural reconciliation.

CONTEXT

From 1960–1996, Guatemala tore itself apart in a civil war between resistance fighters and the military. The fighting claimed 200,000 lives.

EXILE

Rigoberta Menchú was only 20 when she rebelled and joined her father's political movement, the Committee for Peasant Unity. She received death threats and lived in hiding for several months before leaving for exile in Mexico in 1981.

TRAGEDY

Rigoberta Menchú's family suffered greatly during the civil war: one of her brothers was brutally murdered; her father was imprisoned several times before being killed during a demonstration; and her mother was arrested, tortured, and murdered.

AWARD

In 1992, at age 33, Rigoberta Menchú became the youngest ever winner of the Nobel Peace Prize. Her award was in recognition of her work in support of indigenous peoples.

NOBEL

She was the first
indigenous person
to be awarded the
Nobel Peace Prize.

COSTUME

Deeply proud of her
roots, she wears
traditional Mayan
costume.

GUATEMALAN FLAG

In Guatemala,
the Maya account for about
40% of the population.

The Mayan conscience

Jody Williams

IDENTITY

Professor

American

Born on October 9, 1950, in Brattleboro, VT

During the 1980s, American Jody Williams studied international relations. Traveling to El Salvador and Nicaragua, countries devastated by war, she saw firsthand the terrible destruction that anti-personnel mines caused. In 1992, she launched the International Campaign to Ban Landmines (ICBL), which led to the Ottawa Convention, a disarmament treaty signed in December 1997. Today, Jody Williams is waging a new battle against autonomous weapons, known as killer robots.

OTTAWA CONVENTION

This treaty bans the use, production, stockpiling, and trade in anti-personnel landmines. It calls for all existing stocks to be destroyed. So far, 162 countries have signed the Ottawa Convention.

MINEFIELD

Hidden on or under the ground, anti-personnel landmines explode when people walk over them. These undiscriminating weapons are still a threat after a conflict has ended, and they continue to kill and maim a large number of civilians, including children.

AWARD

Jody Williams was awarded the Nobel Peace Prize in 1997 jointly with ICBL, an umbrella body with several members including the charity Handicap International.

> "Anti-personnel mines claim an average of nine victims every day."
>
> Handicap International, 2013

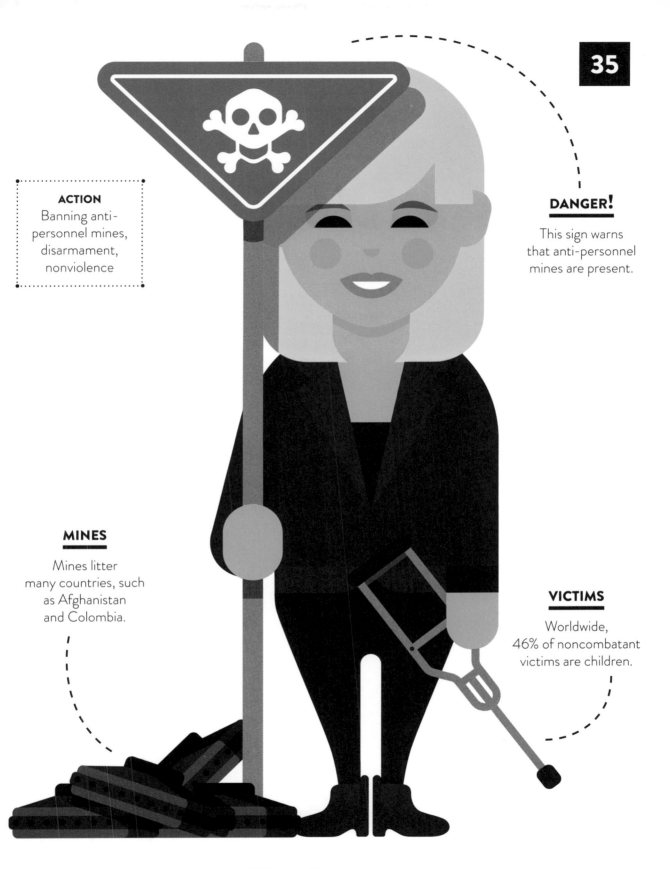

35

ACTION
Banning anti-personnel mines, disarmament, nonviolence

DANGER!
This sign warns that anti-personnel mines are present.

MINES
Mines litter many countries, such as Afghanistan and Colombia.

VICTIMS
Worldwide, 46% of noncombatant victims are children.

The fighter

Daniel Barenboim

World-famous Daniel Barenboim is a pianist and conductor who performs classical music concerts all over the world. A passionate advocate for the political and social role of the arts, he strives to promote peace in the Middle East. He founded the West-Eastern Divan Orchestra in 1999. This symphony orchestra is made up of members from Palestine, Israel, and other countries of the Middle East. Its message promotes dialogue and cooperation between Jews and Arabs.

ALLIANCE

Jewish Argentinian-Israeli musician Daniel Barenboim founded the West-Eastern Divan Orchestra with Christian Palestinian-American intellectual Edward Said.

> "An orchestra is a school for life."
>
> Daniel Barenboim

ACADEMY

In 2016, he opened the Barenboim–Said Academy in Berlin. The academy offers Middle Eastern students a syllabus that combines music with literature, philosophy, and history. It strives to be "a place of hope, an argument for reason and harmony."

IN PALESTINE

Despite the conflict between Palestine and Israel, he is always happy to perform in Palestinian territory, and played in Ramallah in 2005 and Gaza in 2011. In 2008, he accepted the Palestinian passport offered to him.

IDENTITY

Pianist and conductor

Argentinian, naturalized Israeli, Spanish, and Palestinian

Born on November 15, 1942, in Buenos Aires

36

MAESTRO
He has given brilliant performances of works by Beethoven, Mozart, Wagner, Bruckner, and others.

MUSIC
He seeks to promote peace in the Middle East through classical music.

ACTION
Peace in the Middle East, friendship between Israelis and Palestinians

PIANO
A child prodigy, he was just seven when he gave his first piano recital.

Musician without borders

Kim Dae-jung

IDENTITY

President of South Korea

Politician

South Korean

Born on January 6, 1924 (later he had it changed to December 3, 1925), in Hauido

Died on August 18, 2009, in Seoul

Following the Korean War, the young Kim Dae-jung argued in favor of a democratic South Korea. He was then punished by the dictatorial military regime that was in power. After many years of prison and exile, he returned to active politics in 1985 and was elected president in 1998. During his term in office, he worked tirelessly to rebuild his country's economy and revive ties with North Korea. His policy to promote peaceful coexistence between the two Koreas was called the Sunshine Policy.

REPRESSION

In total, he spent six years in prison, three years in exile, and ten years under house arrest. He also survived two assassination attempts!

A RAY OF SUNSHINE

Despite the war having ended, the relationship between the two Koreas remained tense. Anxious to ease tensions, Kim Dae-jung became the first South Korean president to visit North Korea. He met Kim Jong-il there in June 2000.

TWO KOREAS

At the end of World War I, the Korean peninsula was cut in two: North Korea was backed by the Soviet Union, and South Korea by the United States. This division led to the Korean War, which lasted from 1950 to 1953.

AWARD

Kim Dae-jung was awarded the Nobel Peace Prize in 2000 in recognition of his fight for democracy, human rights, peace, and reconciliation on the Korean peninsular.

37

SOUTH KOREAN FLAG

He led South Korea from 1998 to 2003.

ACTION
Democracy, reconciliation between North Korea and South Korea, pacifism

NOBEL PRIZE WINNER

He is often compared to Nelson Mandela, a fellow Nobel Prize winner.

NORTH KOREAN FLAG

North Korea is the most isolated country in the world.

The reconciler

Michael Moore

CONTEXT

Passed in 1791, the Second Amendment to the Constitution of the United States gives every American citizen the right to bear arms.

The left-wing American activist Michael Moore is famous for making documentaries that take a critical look at contemporary American society. In 2002, he turned his attention to the country's frightening problems with firearms, releasing *Bowling for Columbine*. His film looks at America's fascination with guns, their unrestricted sale, the omnipresence of violence, and the climate of fear spread by the media and politicians. Moore claims that all these factors help the powerful American arms industry.

COLUMBINE MASSACRE

Bowling for Columbine refers to the terrible shooting spree that took place on April 20, 1999, in Columbine High School in Littleton, Colorado. Two young male students killed 12 of their fellow pupils and a teacher before killing themselves.

IDENTITY

Filmmaker

American

Born on April 23, 1954, in Flint, MI

THE SCOURGE

In the USA, over 90 people are shot and killed every day (30 murders and 60 suicides). Despite this, and the cries of alarm from Michael Moore and many others, a large section of the US public remains deeply attached to the Second Amendment.

AWARD

Bowling for Columbine won the 55th Anniversary Prize at the 2002 Cannes Film Festival and the Oscar for Best Documentary in 2003.

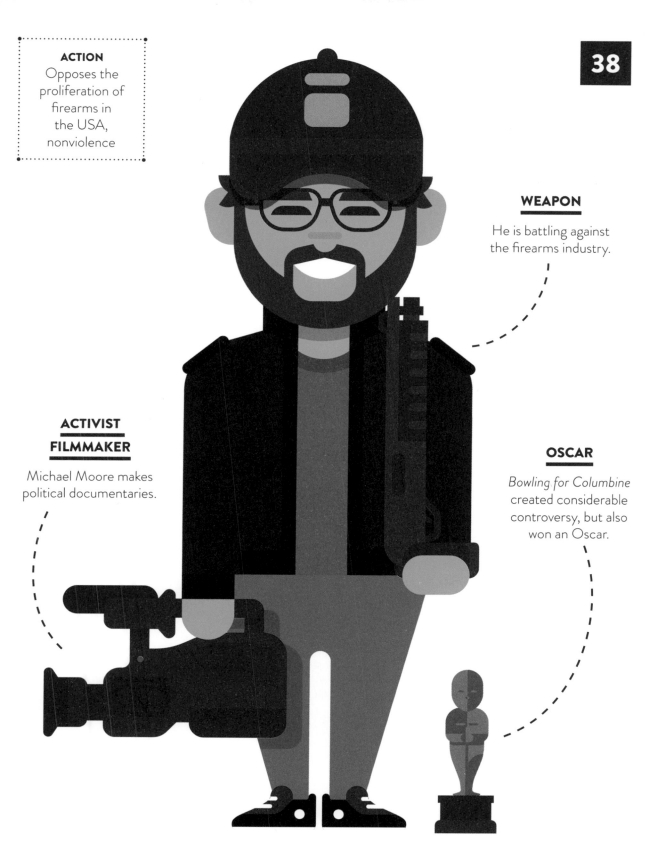

38

ACTION
Opposes the proliferation of firearms in the USA, nonviolence

WEAPON
He is battling against the firearms industry.

ACTIVIST FILMMAKER
Michael Moore makes political documentaries.

OSCAR
Bowling for Columbine created considerable controversy, but also won an Oscar.

The troublemaker

Tegla Loroupe

One of Kenya's all-time greats, in 1994 Tegla Loroupe became the first African woman to win the prestigious New York marathon. She is also a woman of great humanitarian convictions who uses her fame to promote peace and African causes. In 2003, she created the Tegla Loroupe Peace Foundation, which uses sports as a tool to promote friendship between peoples and gender equality. Tegla Loroupe is also a tireless organizer of Peace Marathons that are held throughout east Africa.

FORCE FOR GOOD

Robert Matanda and Julius Arile were two bandits who imposed a reign of terror on northern Kenya. Tegla Loroupe courageously set out to meet them, and persuaded them to lay down their arms. She even managed to get them to take up athletics!

REFUGEES

Tegla Loroupe works with athletes who are living as refugees in Kenyan camps, hosting them at her training center and preparing them for competitions. In 2016, she helped six athletes from South Sudan to compete at the Rio Olympics.

EDUCATION

As a child, she enrolled at school all by herself, defying her father, who would not give his permission. She had to run six miles to and from school every day to attend her classes.

IDENTITY

Athlete, marathon champion

Kenyan

Born on May 9, 1973, in Kutomwony

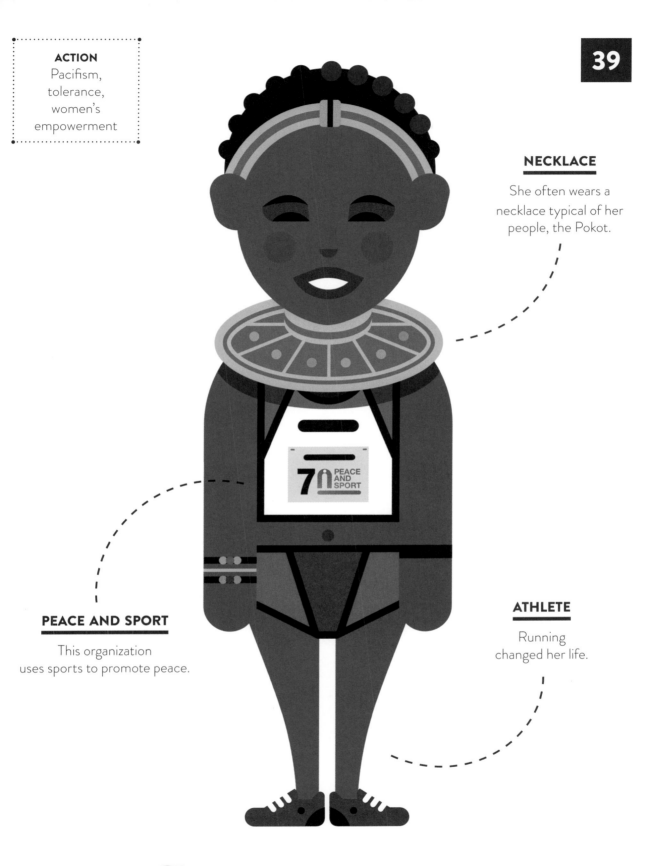

39

ACTION
Pacifism, tolerance, women's empowerment

NECKLACE
She often wears a necklace typical of her people, the Pokot.

PEACE AND SPORT
This organization uses sports to promote peace.

ATHLETE
Running changed her life.

The bighearted athlete

Malala Yousafzai

At the age of 11, the young Pakistani activist Malala Yousafzai resisted the Taliban rule (alongside her father), which forbade girls from receiving an education. Under the pseudonym Gul Makai, she kept a blog about her struggles. Threatened with death several times, she was attacked on October 9, 2012, on her way back from taking an exam. Miraculously, she survived a gunshot wound to her head, and left the country to recover in the United Kingdom. Since then, Malala has continued her own studies... and her fight for education.

> "One child, one teacher, one book, one pen can change the world."
>
> Malala Yousafzai

THE TALIBAN

Malala is from the Swat Valley in Pakistan, which fell under Taliban rule from 2007 to 2009. This fundamentalist movement oppresses women in particular, preventing them from getting an education or having a job.

PRIZE

On October 10, 2014, Pakistan's Malala Yousafzai jointly won the Nobel Peace Prize with India's Kailash Satyarthi.

UNITED NATIONS

On July 12th 2013 – her 16th birthday – Malala gave a speech to the UN forum advocating education for all, and on April 10th 2017, she was appointed the youngest-ever United Nations Messenger of Peace.

IDENTITY

Activist for the education of girls

Pakistani

Born on 12th July, 1997, in Mingora.

40

DRESS

Malala wears a salwar kameez and headscarf – the traditional dress of Pakistan.

NOBEL

Malala was the youngest Nobel Peace Prize winner, aged just 17.

ACTION
The right to education for all, especially girls and young women

HER BOOK

I Am Malala: The Girl Who Stood Up for Education and Was Shot by the Taliban

The courageous student

Timeline

REVOLUTIONS OF **1848**

The wind of revolution blows across Europe. In France, Victor Schoelcher engineers the abolition of slavery.

INTERNATIONAL PEACE CONGRESS, PARIS

In response to the wars that broke out in Europe throughout the 19th century, Victor Hugo advocates a united and fraternal Europe.

CREATION OF THE LN (LEAGUE OF NATIONS)

Woodrow Wilson is the driving force behind this international organization, created with the goal of maintaining world peace.

WORLD WAR II

Resistance activists Sophie Scholl and Raoul Wallenberg oppose the Nazi barbarity.

PEACEFUL MARCH ON WASHINGTON

Martin Luther King fights racial segregation and calls for equal civil rights.

VIETNAM WAR

Activist singers Joan Baez and John Lennon denounce the conflict.

CREATION OF THE NOBEL PEACE PRIZE

———

Henri Dunant, founder of the Red Cross, wins the first Nobel Peace Prize.

WORLD WAR I

———

Pacifists Jean Jaurès (French) and Rosa Luxemburg (German) oppose the war.

CREATION OF THE UN (UNITED NATIONS)

———

Eleanor Roosevelt presents the Universal Declaration of Human Rights.

INDEPENDENCE OF INDIA AND PAKISTAN

———

A leading figure of the decolonization movement, Mohandas Gandhi chooses the path of passive resistance and nonviolence.

FIRST EARTH SUMMIT

———

Environmental activist Wangari Maathai fights against deforestation in Africa.

FALL OF THE BERLIN WALL

———

Mikhail Gorbachev helps to end the Cold War.

Inspiring | Educating | Creating | Entertaining

Brimming with creative inspiration, how-to projects, and useful
information to enrich your everyday life, Quarto Knows is a favorite
destination for those pursuing their interests and passions. Visit our
site and dig deeper with our books into your area of interest:
Quarto Creates, Quarto Cooks, Quarto Homes, Quarto Lives,
Quarto Drives, Quarto Explores, Quarto Gifts, or Quarto Kids.

A catalog record for this book is available from the British Library.

ISBN 978-1-78603-144-0

The illustrations were created digitally
Set in Brandon Grotesque and Gotham Rounded

Manufactured in Singapore CO082020

9 8 7 6 5 4 3

Collect the rest in the series!

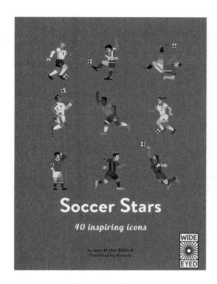

Soccer Stars
978-1-78603-142-6

Greek Gods & Heroes
978-1-78603-143-3

Music Legends
978-1-78603-145-7

Black Music Greats
978-1-78603-471-7

Super Scientists
978-1-78603-474-8

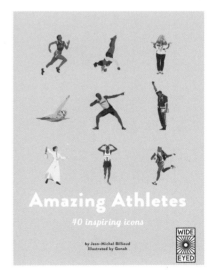

Amazing Athletes
978-0-7112-5254-7